Retail

NAJOUD ENSAFF
AND ANNE ROONEY

THANK YOU FOR SHOPPING
AT
ASDA
Happy to Help
Right price
Please take one
celebration
Happy
Christmas!
ASDA
Please take one
ASDA
Christmas
SORTED!

Contents

The World of Retail

Retail – selling goods to customers – is a huge and vibrant industry. In the UK and Northern Ireland, over three million people work in retail – one in ten of the working population. They work in big and small businesses, ranging from independent shops and high-street stores, through supermarkets and large retail parks, to superstores and giant international chains. Not all retail outlets are shops – market stalls, online retailers, shopping catalogues and auctioneers are all retail businesses. Within these different settings there are many roles and opportunities demanding a wide variety of skills and personalities.

TO WORK IN RETAIL, YOU WILL NEED

- *to work well in a team*
- *to have an interest in selling and goods*
- *to enjoy working with people*
- *to be customer focused*

RETAIL – IT'S NOT JUST SELLING

The public face of retail is the sales assistants and management staff you see in stores when you go shopping, but there is far more to the world of retail. If you enjoy working with people, you might like to deal directly with customers on the shop floor, or work in human resources. If you like to work with numbers,

Department stores such as Macy's in New York City employ a vast number of people in retail jobs, including managers, buyers and sales assistants.

you could choose the financial side of retail, or managing and controlling stock (goods to sell). If you like design and have a good 'eye' you might produce window displays or design the website of an online store. Or you might like to work in buying, choosing new products to sell. Whichever area you decide to make your career in, you will be aiming – with the rest of the team you work with – towards increasing sales and profit for your organisation.

Retail outlets include independent shops, such as this bakery in Jerusalem, Israel. Employees of smaller operations may be promoted quickly but they need to have a mature and responsible attitude towards their work.

GOODS FOR SALE

Retail is all about selling. If you choose to work in retail you might sell fresh food or designer fashion, e-books or cars or anything in between. You will need to be passionate about the products you work with as you must really believe they are the best if you are to persuade people to buy them. Choosing the area of retail you want to work in is as important as deciding on the role you want.

SUIT YOURSELF

When choosing a job and retail sector, you need to think about your own personality, interests and strengths. Are you good at looking at an overall plan, at analysing a problem, or at dealing face-to-face with people? Are you good with numbers? Do you have an eye for detail? Are you creative, with lots of ideas? Are you a well-organised person? Do you like to travel? Are you happy working shifts? Knowing what skills you have will help you to find an area and a role that suit you.

FINDING A JOB

Jobs in retail are advertised in the media and online, and in specialist magazines and newspapers. When you are starting out, perhaps looking for a weekend or holiday job, the easiest way to find a position is to look for vacancies advertised in shop windows or go into a shop you like and ask.

On the Shop Floor

The most obvious aspect of retail is selling to the public in a shop. This is an environment we are all familiar with from our everyday lives, and most people don't give much thought to what is involved in it. The work carried out in shops or other retail outlets is called 'store operations'.

RETAIL MANAGER

Every store has a manager who is responsible for its day-to-day running. In a large organisation with more than one store, there is a management chain, up to head office. The manager of a large store will have help from assistants and managers of different departments or floors. In a smaller shop, the manager will personally take on a wider range of tasks and responsibilities.

A store manager is responsible for the smooth running of the shop. He or she must make sure that there is enough stock of the right type properly displayed, that there are trained staff on hand, that the premises open on time and are clean, well-run and welcoming to customers and that the store meets its targets and is profitable.

Managers of large supermarkets must ensure that communication between different areas is effective and that customers are treated well.

MAIN TASKS – STORE MANAGER

- *ensuring the store is attractive and that staff give customers a good service*
- *monitoring staff progress*
- *checking stock and staffing levels*
- *deciding on and meeting sales targets*
- *liaising with senior managers*
- *monitoring staff progress*
- *ensuring health and safety regulations are met*

Store managers are responsible for making sure that high standards of health and sanitation are maintained.

MANAGING PEOPLE

Managers may be responsible for recruiting and training staff, for organising work schedules and shifts, and for handling any disciplinary matters relating to staff. They are involved in setting targets for their staff and monitoring their progress. Motivating staff and dealing with their problems can be a particularly rewarding part of working with people. In a large organisation, a human resources department will help with recruiting, training and disciplining staff, but day-to-day staff management is still the responsibility of the store manager.

BUSINESS MANAGEMENT

A manager must set targets for the business and make sure they are achieved. This usually means setting and meeting sales figures. To achieve targets, the manager must make the shop and its stock attractive to customers so that they come in and spend money. In many cases, the manager oversees selecting and buying stock, and advertising or promoting the store.

HANDY HINT

You are more likely to win a place on a management trainee programme if you can gain some experience in a retail environment. There are often temporary or part-time jobs available in shops and restaurants, which you can do while you are still at school or college. This will help you to choose the area of retail that most interests you, and will show employers that you have made an informed choice and have genuine enthusiasm.

LIFE AS A RETAIL MANAGER

Managers usually spend some time each day walking the shop floor, checking the displays and stock and making sure customers are well served. The manager also has overall responsibility for health and safety, and for making sure the business is run legally. This requires knowledge of the law and of financial practices.

Managers in small stores usually have a more hands-on role and more independence than those in chain stores (or retail multiples) such as Walmart or Marks & Spencer. In a large retail chain, functions such as recruitment, stock selection and promotion are carried out by specialist staff at head office.

Store managers in a retail chain are in close contact with senior managers at head office or regional level, and need to make sure their store is run and develops in line with national strategies.

TO WORK AS A RETAIL MANAGER, YOU WILL NEED

- *strong leadership and organisational skills*
- *good communication skills*
- *the ability to prioritise and delegate work*
- *the ability to work well under pressure*

Managers of grocery stores must monitor stock supplies and instruct staff to make certain that food does not pass its 'sell-by' date.

LINE MANAGER

Line managers have responsibility for a department or area of the shop, such as household appliances, or the checkouts in a supermarket. The line manager looks after staff, stock and equipment in his or her area, setting staff work rotas, organising re-stocking of shelves, making sure tills are staffed, and that the area is neat, clean and attractive.

The line manager spends much of the day on the shop floor making sure that everything is running smoothly. Line managers often have direct contact with customers, answering queries, dealing with problems and making recommendations. You will need good 'people skills' to be a line manager – the ability to listen sympathetically, to be polite with distressed or angry customers, and to offer constructive solutions to problems. You may also have to deal with difficult situations such as shoplifting or breakages by customers, lost children, and people falling ill or having an accident in the shop.

Kevin – supermarket line manager

'I joined this supermarket chain when I left school, working on the checkouts. It's a large chain, so there are lots of opportunities for in-store training. I showed I was keen and a good worker, so I quickly got on to a fast-track training programme. I became first a team leader and then a line manager. I've just completed a foundation degree while keeping my full-time job. Some people come into the supermarket as graduate trainees, but I wanted to get straight to work and further my education while earning.

'My day-to-day work involves managing the staff working on the checkouts and taking care of all health and safety and customer care issues relating to the checkouts. I organise work rotas, decide when to put out a call for more staff, and I'm the one who has to cope if the technology breaks down. There's never a dull day, and I'm working on progressing my management career at the same time.'

Among other things, supermarket line managers need to deal with problems that arise, such as customer complaints and supply shortages.

PERSONAL SHOPPER

Some stores employ personal shoppers who work with individual customers to meet their needs. A personal shopper advises people on their purchases. He or she might help them to choose an outfit for a particular occasion, or renew their wardrobe for a new season or a change in their life. Personal shoppers often work in fashion departments, but some stores offer the service in furnishings and other areas.

FASHION KNOW-HOW

To be a personal shopper working in fashion, you will need to understand how colours and fabrics work together, know about trends in clothing and fashions, and understand how different styles, cuts and colours suit different body shapes and complexions. You will need a good eye for design and detail.

Personal shoppers need to combine good judgement in colour and fashion with tact and sensitivity towards their clients.

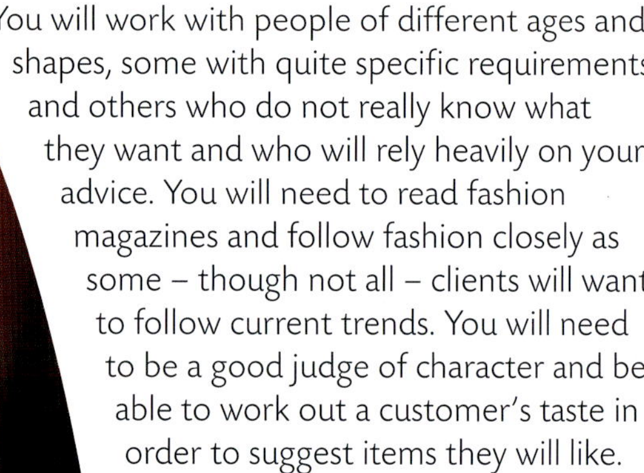

You will work with people of different ages and shapes, some with quite specific requirements and others who do not really know what they want and who will rely heavily on your advice. You will need to read fashion magazines and follow fashion closely as some – though not all – clients will want to follow current trends. You will need to be a good judge of character and be able to work out a customer's taste in order to suggest items they will like.

TO WORK AS A PERSONAL SHOPPER, YOU WILL NEED

- ***a good knowledge of fashion***
- ***an understanding of how colours and fabrics work together and of which styles suit which body types***
- ***good interpersonal and communication skills***

Personal shoppers who work in-house must be very knowledgeable about the store's merchandise and able to describe it in a clear and appealing way.

WHO PAYS?

Personal shoppers who work for a large store are paid by the store. The service may be offered free to shoppers, or they may pay a fee to be kept up to date with new lines or products. If you work in-house in a store, you will need to know the product range of the store very well. You will be recommending items from the store's full range, and will need to be able to put together outfits using items and accessories from different departments.

Some personal shoppers work freelance and choose items from a number of different stores. In this case, the customer pays a fee directly to the personal shopper. Some people prefer to use freelance personal shoppers as their advice is impartial – they are not bound to recommend items from one store, but can pick from any number of outlets.

There is a growing number of online personal shoppers who source items for customers from online stores. They carry out product research and price comparison on any type of goods, then advise the customer of the best buys. This is usually a freelance career.

HANDY HINT

As with anyone working freelance, personal shoppers have to keep track of their income and spending so that they can do their accounts correctly and work within the law.

CUSTOMER SERVICES MANAGER

The customer services department in a retail organisation deals with enquiries and complaints. Sometimes customers will be upset or angry, so it takes tact and patience to work successfully in customer services. The manager of a customer services desk or department will often be called in to give a final decision on problems, or to solve particular problems that are not covered by company guidelines. The customer services manager has responsibility for the safety of staff, making sure they are not attacked or abused by angry customers.

Customer services managers need to be good listeners and to have 'people skills' so that they can respond effectively to customer enquiries and complaints.

GETTING IT RIGHT

The public image of a company often relies on how well the customer services department deals with problems. Customers who are not satisfied with their treatment may complain to customer protection organisations, the media or use the internet, Twitter or other technologies to make their frustration public. This can be very damaging to the organisation – but it can be avoided by good customer relations staff.

You may be involved in developing customer services policy in discussion with management and legal advisers. You will need to implement any new policies and train staff in new procedures, as well as monitor the performance of the department and check customer satisfaction.

TO WORK AS A CUSTOMER SERVICES MANAGER, YOU WILL NEED

- ***good communication skills***
- ***to be diplomatic and patient***
- ***the ability to remain polite when dealing with customers who are upset or angry***

IS THE CUSTOMER ALWAYS RIGHT?

Customers are protected by consumer protection laws which state that anything they buy must be safe, must be fit for its intended purpose, and must work properly. In addition, many retail organisations offer extra guarantees or extended warranties on goods, or allow customers to exchange things if they change their mind about a purchase. If you work as a customer services manager you will need to know the law about consumer purchases and your organisation's policy on exchanges and faulty goods.

You will need a good knowledge of the product range – sometimes people will think an item is faulty when they are actually using it wrongly. Occasionally, a customer may claim something was faulty when they bought it but it is clear that they have broken it. Dealing with tricky situations like this while remaining polite is a challenging and rewarding part of customer services.

In a store, members of the customer services team work with customers face to face, but in other retail organisations customer support may be carried out over the phone, or by email.

MAIN TASKS – CUSTOMER SERVICES MANAGER

- *running a customer service desk or department*
- *giving help and advice to customers face to face, over the telephone, or by email*
- *investigating and solving customers' problems and complaints*
- *issuing refunds, exchanges or compensation*
- *arranging services for customers*
- *developing feedback and complaints procedures*
- *recruiting and training staff*

If a customer wants to exchange an item, staff need to be polite and helpful.

Buying and Selling

All retail businesses work by buying in stock and selling it on to customers at a higher price. Two very important aspects of this process are ordering the right stock in the first place and persuading people to buy it.

TO BECOME A BUYER, YOU WILL NEED

- *a strong commercial awareness*
- *an understanding of what motivates customers to buy products*
- *good analytical skills*
- *creativity and the ability to predict future trends*

RETAIL BUYER

If a shop is to succeed it needs to stock goods that customers want to buy. It is the job of a buyer to find just the right items. Buyers usually specialise in a particular type of product, such as toys, fashion accessories, electrical goods, books, or music. They build up expertise in their field, and develop detailed knowledge of the market, including all the suppliers, the various methods of manufacture, and the different areas of the market. For example, someone who specialises in buying luggage will need to know the difference between luxury products and value ranges, how luggage made from leather and luggage made from artificial materials differs, and which will suit the customers of a particular store.

A retail buyer and a seller negotiate terms at a trade fair in China.

A buyer assesses a range of menswear in advance of a fashion show in London, UK.

FINDING THE BEST – WHEREVER IT MAY BE

Buyers often have to travel to visit suppliers, trade fairs and shows where they can see new products coming on to the market, compare prices and quality, and choose which items to buy. They may need to go to the factories where goods are made to check standards. It is not just a matter of making sure the product is good enough. Many retailers today have responded to public pressure to make sure that their goods are ethically sourced and produced. Buyers may need to check that workers in a garment factory or farm are fairly treated and work in a safe environment, as this may be a condition of the store's contract with the supplier.

A buyer may work in a store, or from the head office of a retail chain. Working in a store, a buyer might have to schedule visits from prospective suppliers who want to come and show their range in the hope of getting a contract. The buyer needs to know what customers will buy and the prices they will be prepared to pay. Buyers look at computerised records of sales to see what has sold well in the past, and combine this with their experience of the market and new trends to decide which product lines the store should stock.

MAIN TASKS – RETAIL BUYER

- *choosing products and ranges*
- *placing supplier orders and negotiating contracts*
- *analysing trends and consumer buying patterns*
- *attending shows or trade fairs to find new products and suppliers*
- *evaluating product quality*
- *presenting collections to senior retail managers*

SPECIAL KNOWLEDGE

Some areas require specialist knowledge and also change rapidly. Fashion buyers, for instance, go to fashion shows and watch developing trends so that they can judge what will be popular in coming months. Other areas that require specialist knowledge include wine, antiques, cars, motorbikes and consumer electronics. In fields like this, it is important to have a genuine interest in the product range.

In a small store, the buyer may need to deal with a range of different types of products, or with all the products the store stocks.

CHANGING MARKETS

A buyer needs to be able to keep up with trends in consumer purchasing and predict the direction in which trends are likely to go. Buyers also need to notice and respond quickly to changes in spending patterns among shoppers.

Picking objects that are likely to be popular as Christmas presents, or the latest fashion in clothes takes practice and a real feel for the market. When a buyer gets it right, the store can make a large profit – but mistakes can be very expensive, so it's a big responsibility. Buyers choose stock many months ahead of it being in the store, so are always thinking a couple of seasons ahead, choosing Christmas items in summer for example.

Two women are drawn to the clothes on display in a shop window in Milan, Italy. The success or failure of a store depends on the choices made by retail buyers.

Kairi – retail buyer

'I work as the buyer for a small chain of gift shops in airports. Much of our produce has a patriotic theme, and some of it is perishable – foodstuffs such as smoked salmon and sweets. I choose all the items that are stocked in our outlets. Some of them come from very small suppliers – craftsmen and women working on their own or in a small co-operative – while others are produced by huge manufacturers. I have to negotiate prices, keep track of stock and analyse sales figures so that I know what is selling and what is not – there's no point in taking more of something that is very hard to shift.

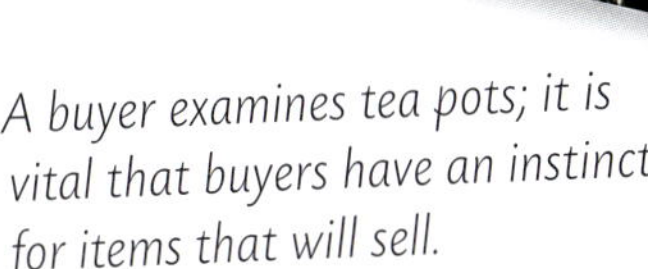

A buyer examines tea pots; it is vital that buyers have an instinct for items that will sell.

'Some of the items we sell are made to our own designs. I find this aspect of the job most exciting, as I work with designers and producers to make something that is unique. These specialist products are based on what I believe will sell, from my knowledge of the market and analysis of our sales figures. I have to find suppliers and work closely with them through all stages of the process.

'Generally, I have a good relationship with suppliers we use a lot so I enjoy visiting them and showing them around our stores when they come to see how the merchandise is displayed. I feel I've something to be proud of in a well-stocked outlet that sees a lot of customer footfall.'

WINDOW DRESSER

A window dresser makes attractive displays of stock in a window, with the aim of making the shop appeal to passing customers so that they go inside. Window dressers might have to put together special themed displays (for Christmas, for instance) or promote a particular range or type of stock. Clothes shops and department stores often put a lot of effort into building attractive window displays and changing them frequently. Window dressing is part of visual merchandising, the field which covers all aspects of displaying goods and making a store attractive and easy for customers to navigate.

A dresser arranges motorised puppets in the window of a Paris department store.

FINDING A JOB

There are some qualifications in retail display, but most people start with a job in retail and then move into window dressing. Training in interior design is a good starting point, too. Most window dressers learn on the job and move into the work when they are already employed by a store.

TO BECOME A WINDOW DRESSER, YOU WILL NEED

- ***an eye for colour, and for textures and shapes that go well together***
- ***retail experience***
- ***imagination and enthusiasm***
- ***physical fitness – you'll be moving things around and spending all day on your feet***

Andrew – window dresser

'I work as a window dresser in a large department store in central London. It's a creative job – you need enthusiasm and flair. We have more than 100 metres of windows and change the displays every few weeks. Changing a display takes two full days – one to move the old display out and clean the windows, then another to build the new display. There is also time in between spent working on the design and sourcing the items from around the store. The theme is set by management, but within that I have quite a lot of freedom to brief my team. I work out the designs, and some other members of the team do most of the arranging and picking items to include – I do a bit of that, too, as it helps me keep up-to-date with what's in the store.

'As well as the main window displays, we do little displays inside the store. These are important to customers as they act as signposts to different departments – they can see a display from the escalator and think 'ah yes, there are the shoes . . . ' and head off in the right direction.

A jungle-themed Christmas window display in a department store in New York City.

'I work Monday to Friday, as Saturday is too busy to be standing on ladders making displays, and the shop has to look its best then. Some stores do it differently, and only change displays when the shop is closed so the hours are anti-social then.

'I love the job – there's always something new to do. The best thing is seeing customers outside gawping at a new display and pointing out to each other the bits they like best. That really raises my spirits.'

PUBLIC RELATIONS OFFICER

Public relations (PR) is part of marketing a business or product. Working in PR involves helping to create, maintain and promote a company's public image and profile. As a PR officer you will think of ways to publicise the retail organisation. You might also be involved in organising events to bring more customers into the shop, such as product launches, openings of new stores, book signings, visits from celebrities and so on. You may have to brief journalists and organise advertising.

A POSITIVE IMAGE

People working in PR help to keep a retailer's brand name in the public eye. Jobs involve liaising with the media, writing press releases and organising publicity campaigns. PR involves using new media to reach the retailer's target audience. This can include podcasts, websites, social networking sites and company blogs, so you will need to keep up-to-date with current trends in technology. If you work in PR, you may need to speak in public, give radio or television interviews and talk to the press. You may work alongside advertising agency staff to devise promotions, loyalty card schemes and other ways of boosting customers' interest in the store.

DEALING WITH TROUBLE

When there is a news story about a product, such as a question about product safety, it is the PR department that organises the release of information to the media. It is important to balance customer safety and information with maintaining the store's good name.

TO BECOME A PR MANAGER, YOU WILL NEED

- ***good time-management skills***
- ***confidence talking to journalists and others in the media***
- ***the ability to communicate effectively and persuasively in person and on paper***

Public relations officers sometimes recruit famous names to help promote their products.

Tom – PR manager

'I work for a mobile phone retailer and my main responsibilities are to promote the company's image and communicate positively with the media. I got into PR after university. I chose to do a degree in public relations and, as part of my degree, I had to do a work placement in a company. Luckily they liked me and offered me a job after my degree, so I stayed on.

Public relations managers need to have excellent communication skills, both written and spoken. They must have the confidence to speak in public, when required.

'On a day-to-day basis my job entails dealing with all the enquiries we receive. I also oversee the marketing of the chain of retail stores and its products through press releases and brochures. There's a lot of focus on deadlines, so being able to manage your time well is important in this job. I liaise with journalists who request information or interviews, and communicate directly with our PR agency. Usually I work between 9.00 a.m. and 5.30 p.m. but when we have big projects I work longer hours. We're just working towards a set of promotions and a brochure, so things will get busy as the launch date nears.

'I enjoy my job because of the interaction I have with people. It can get really busy sometimes, especially when we're working to tight deadlines, but I find this stimulating.'

The Supply Chain

Getting goods into the shops is a large part of retailing, though it's one people don't usually think about when it runs smoothly. The supply chain is the sequence of steps, people and businesses involved in moving goods from producers to shops.

SUPPLY CHAIN MANAGER

A supply chain manager is responsible for making sure the process of supplying goods to shops runs smoothly. The job can involve sourcing and purchasing goods, together with logistics, transportation, warehousing and storage, and distribution (sending goods out to stores).

THE RIGHT THINGS IN THE RIGHT PLACE AT THE RIGHT TIME

Often, a retail chain orders stock from a wholesaler (a business that supplies in bulk), although some large chains deal directly with manufacturers or farmers. A large order of stock is moved – or shipped – to the retailer's warehouse, then sent out to shops when it is needed. It is important to judge the stock level to hold in the warehouse and in stores correctly. Keeping unsold stock ties up space and money and reduces profit, but running out of popular items can also be an expensive mistake.

Some organisations run a 'just in time' stock system, which means they order stock just in time to send it out again. This system depends on precise timing and good judgement so that shops do not run out of vital stock. High quality information about customers' buying patterns and sophisticated computerised stock control systems make this possible.

MAIN TASKS – SUPPLY CHAIN MANAGER

- *setting and monitoring levels of stock*
- *managing the shipment of goods*
- *making sure targets are met*
- *logistics*
- *warehouse management*
- *improving supply networks*

Supply chain managers keep computerised records of the huge quantities of stock in their warehouse.

Supply chain managers decide on the best methods of transportation for their products.

SUPPLY AND DEMAND

The demand for many goods changes with the seasons, weather or the state of the economy. The supply chain manager has to assess demand ahead of time, and this is not always easy. When there is a wet, cold summer, for instance, many shops are left with stock of barbecues and other hot-weather items. A surprise Christmas hit can leave shops sold out of a popular item, so losing sales. In fashion and fresh foods, correctly judging stock levels is important all the time.

LOGISTICS

Logistics involves working out how to get goods from one place to another and managing their flow. Logistics are often handled by a supply chain manager, though some organisations have separate logistics managers. The work involves using computers and liaising with many other people. If you work in this area, you may have to decide on methods of transport (air, sea, rail or road) and manage the stocking and layout of warehouses to make the movement of goods in and out as efficient as possible.

FINDING A JOB

A foundation degree in logistics, transport management, geography, international transport or supply chain management will give you a good start. There are also NVQs in Distribution, Warehousing and Storage Operations or Integrated Logistics Support. The Chartered Institute of Logistics and Transport (CILT UK) has information about advanced diplomas in transport and logistics.

WAREHOUSE AND STOCK MANAGER

After goods have been bought from a producer or wholesaler, they are stored in a warehouse until they have to be sent out to a shop. Warehousing is an important stage in retailing. The warehouse and stock must be properly managed so that shops can be supplied promptly.

In larger organisations, warehouse management and stock control are separate tasks, but in smaller organisations the warehouse manager may also carry out stock control.

MANAGING A WAREHOUSE

The warehouse manager is responsible for the day-to-day running of the warehouse, safe storage of stock, and maintenance of all vehicles, machinery and equipment. It is the manager's job to plan requirements for storage and equipment and make sure all stock is properly and securely handled and stored. The manager must make sure all staff are trained and follow health and safety guidelines in their work, as a warehouse can be a dangerous environment in which to work.

At this supermarket warehouse, goods are loaded directly on to trucks by way of conveyor belts.

TO BECOME A WAREHOUSE AND STOCK MANAGER, YOU WILL NEED

- *good management skills*
- *physical fitness*
- *an understanding of the stock and its transport and storage requirements*
- *knowledge of health and safety issues and practices*

Most warehouses use automated and computerised systems. If you work as a warehouse manager you will need to be confident with these systems as you will have to produce reports and statistical charts for head office.

The warehousing of perishable stock such as fresh food is particularly challenging. The warehouse manager must make sure the levels of temperature and humidity are suitable, and that the oldest stock leaves the warehouse first so that none has a chance to deteriorate or spoil.

STOCK CONTROL

Stock control involves controlling the flow of stock both into and out of the warehouse. The warehouse manager may be responsible for managing stock control staff. Stock control involves checking incoming shipments of goods, organising their storage and having them moved to the right place in the warehouse. Stock must be properly labelled and stored so that it can be found easily. Most stock controllers use hand-held scanners to read barcodes on goods moving in and out of the warehouse and between locations. The computerised stock control system is automatically updated with stock levels and locations. When the till in a store reads a barcode on an item, the stock control system is updated. In this way, the store and the warehouse communicate so that sold goods can be quickly replaced.

MAIN TASKS – WAREHOUSE AND STOCK MANAGER

- *managing staff who work in the warehouse*
- *planning and securing storage*
- *supplying and maintaining equipment and vehicles*
- *managing the premises, ensuring security and suitable storage conditions*
- *organising staff training*
- *tracking and managing stock movement*
- *producing reports and liaising with head office*
- *dealing with suppliers and haulage companies*

In such a vast space as a warehouse, stock control and monitoring is all-important.

Behind the Scenes

There are many jobs behind the scenes in a shop or other retail outlet. You might not give any thought to these when you go shopping yourself, but if you are thinking about a career in retail you will find that plenty of interesting opportunities are not on the shop floor. Some of these are jobs that exist in many sectors and involve transferable skills, but you may choose to work at them in retail because it is a lively, vibrant environment.

HUMAN RESOURCES MANAGER

The human resources (HR) team deals with recruiting, developing and retaining staff. It helps managers by advising them on human resources policies and putting systems in place to help managers develop their own staff.

HR managers are responsible for all aspects of staffing. They monitor absences, manage risks, and organise staff training and development. They are often involved in recruiting new staff, or overseeing the recruitment officers who do this. HR managers need to be familiar with employment law and company policies and procedures. They may need to visit departments within the company and get to know the staffing issues they face. If you are considering this as a career, you need to develop good people skills and analytical abilities.

Human resources managers need to ensure that companies employ the right balance of staff in terms of skills and experience.

An important part of a human resources manager's job is to interview and select suitable employees.

FINDING A JOB

Many retailers offer employees entry into human resources roles with on-the-job training, and most organisations also provide the opportunity to study towards some form of personnel qualification. This means that you learn the job and work towards a qualification at the same time.

TO BECOME A HUMAN RESOURCES MANAGER, YOU WILL NEED

- ***knowledge of employment law***
- ***good communication skills***
- ***problem-solving abilities***
- ***analytical and people skills***

SOLVING PROBLEMS

An important part of the human resources manager's job is dealing with any disputes and disciplinary matters. Sometimes these relate to sensitive issues such as discrimination, sexual harassment or bullying, so the HR manager needs to be tactful and sensitive.

RECRUITMENT

Recruitment involves finding the right person with the appropriate skills and qualifications to fill each job. The needs of a company must be matched with the skills of a job seeker. A recruitment officer needs to be a good judge of character and have a good understanding of the structure, culture and ethos of the organisation. Anyone working in recruitment must be able to pick staff with not only the right qualifications and experience, but also the qualities to do the job well and fit in with the organisation and other staff. It is important to know and follow equal opportunities law and policies when recruiting staff.

WORKING WITH PEOPLE

Once staff are in place, their professional development is the responsibility of the HR manager. Staff training and assessment, review meetings, incentive schemes, and motivation are all handled by the HR manager and his or her team. When members of staff leave, the HR manager usually interviews them to find out why. The results of these interviews can help the organisation to improve conditions and retain future staff.

ICT SPECIALIST

Like many sectors, retail depends increasingly on computer technology to run smoothly. Computers are used to operate payroll and other aspects of finance, to produce all kinds of documents and presentations, to run stock control systems linked to computerised tills, and in many other areas. Tills, barcode scanners and even the equipment that controls the temperature and humidity are all computerised. If you want to work in ICT, there are many opportunities within retail to put your skills to good use.

WEB DESIGN

Most retailers have a website, and for online retailers such as Amazon it is the core of their business. Working on a retailer's website can involve the use of design and graphics, producing animations or Flash movies, adding sound and videos or working on large, complex databases and e-commerce systems.

KEEPING THINGS GOING

Large computer networks need a comprehensive systems support team to keep them running properly. If you work in systems support, you could be fitting together hardware (installing new terminals, for example), installing or writing software, training users or giving them technical support, or designing or sourcing new software or hardware. You may need to work anti-social hours, and you may need to travel between sites.

TO WORK IN ICT, YOU WILL NEED

- ***good technical skills***
- ***experience with a range of hardware and software***
- ***communication skills, as you will need to deal with non-technical staff and explain complex matters to them***

Companies with complex computer networks will have a team of ICT experts to maintain and update the system.

FINANCE SPECIALIST

A career in retail finance will mean you are helping the organisation to find money to run, develop its business and plan for the future. You may be involved in analysing financial figures, measuring performance and making strategic recommendations. You might analyse the success of a product promotion or look at how well certain stores are performing. There are many departments that need people trained in finance, including purchasing, payroll and accounts.

TO WORK IN FINANCE, YOU WILL NEED

- *to be good with figures*
- *a clear understanding of how business operates*
- *the ability to explain technical information clearly*
- *good analytical skills*

Souad – business development analyst

'I studied business at university, specialising in finance in my last year. During my placement year I worked in retail, in store management, and after graduation I worked for the same company for a year. I gained some great experience related to shop refitting and staff issues but I wasn't using my financial skills and I wanted to. As I lived near an Asda superstore and the company had a good reputation, it seemed the obvious choice.

'I applied to Asda's graduate programme, picking a financial route. I've studied towards the CIMA qualification and am now a business development analyst supporting the promotional and pricing team.

'I enjoy working for a big company. It's allowed me to use my financial skills and has provided me with a good career path, and many financial benefits – I've even become a Walmart shareholder.'

A business development analyst needs to be able to explain financial strategies in a clear and concise way.

Neil – auctioneer

'I deal in antique toys. I identify them and describe them in a catalogue which is sent out to a list of clients and available to anyone else who might want to buy. I work with regular suppliers, but also pick things up at fairs and charity shops. We put the items on display a week before the sale so that people can see them and ask any questions.

'The auction itself gives me a real buzz. The room is crowded, there are phone lines for phone bidders and a video link for online bidders. It's a performance – you have to get people to relax and get them into the rhythm of the sale. And it's important not to talk so quickly that people don't understand what you're saying. Some people come from abroad to buy, so English is not their first language. Speaking slowly and clearly helps them.

'In the lead-up to a sale, I often have to research the items I'm selling – find out where they were made, how old they are, what they're worth, who might have used them. . . This information goes into the catalogue. And then sometimes a buyer will ask another question and I'll have to do more research. It's rewarding and challenging – it can turn into a bit of detective work sometimes.

This auctioneer is conducting a sale of items from a country house. He will be qualified in a relevant subject, such as art history.

'It's very rewarding when someone comes along with something they suspect is a bit of old junk and it turns out to be really valuable or important. They don't always go on to sell it. Some people decide to keep an item that has a bit of a history.'

SALES EXECUTIVE FOR AN ONLINE RETAILER

Online shopping is a growing sector of retail. In some areas, online sales are now a significant part of the market. The biggest difference for people working in online retail is that they do not come into direct contact with customers, and the website takes the place of the shop.

A sales executive for an online retailer may explore new and innovative ways of reaching customers and recruiting business partners to work with the retailer. Online retailers and suppliers can work closely together without the movement of physical stock – the retailer provides a 'shop front' for goods, and when a customer orders them the supplier ships them. Many online retailers also have warehouses of stock, but electronic communication replaces stock movement increasingly.

Some products sold in online stores do not exist as physical objects. The role of a sales executive working with virtual products such as music, video or software delivered by download is very different from that of someone working in sales in a real shop. Even so, the principles of marketing and sales, the financial transactions involved and the customer psychology are much the same. A sales executive working in online retail needs an expert knowledge of the product range and customers' requirements, just as he or she would in a traditional retail environment.

TO WORK AS AN ONLINE SALES EXECUTIVE, YOU WILL NEED,

- *excellent computer skills*
- *an innovative approach*
- *experience in sales or retail*

Sales executives working for online retailers such as Amazon can quickly build up profiles of customer buying patterns.

CALL CENTRE MANAGER

Call centre staff work with telephones to offer customer support or sell to customers. Customer support call centres deal with customers' questions and problems. Often, selling from a call centre is 'cold calling' – phoning people who have not previously expressed an interest in a product or service. The call centre manager is responsible for the staff, the equipment and the smooth running of the call centre.

TO BE A CALL CENTRE MANAGER, YOU WILL NEED

- ***a good telephone manner and communication skills***
- ***tact and patience***
- ***management skills***
- ***to be able to perform well under pressure***

KNOWING THE PRODUCT

Many call centres run help lines for electronic products such as computers and mobile phones. The staff – including the call centre manager – need a very good understanding of the products they are supporting or selling and the types of problems customers may have with them. They need to be able to explain technical information to people who do not have any expert knowledge, and talk customers through instructions clearly and calmly in small steps. If you work as a call centre manager, you will have to take over when a customer is not satisfied with or does not understand the support he or she gets from a call centre worker, or when a call is too complicated for the member of staff who has taken the call.

Call centre managers must be able to cope well with the demands of a stressful environment.

Call centre workers should have a polite and friendly telephone manner. They must remain calm even if their customers do not!

STAFF SUPPORT

The call centre manager is responsible for training and motivating staff, setting targets for calls made or answered, and for monitoring staff progress and setting work rotas. In a large call centre, there will be team leaders who provide first-line support to staff working the phone lines, and these team leaders will report to the call centre manager.

Working in a call centre can be stressful for staff, so the manager needs to provide strong support. Customers who are disappointed with a product or service or who feel their problems are not being dealt with sometimes get angry and aggressive. People who have been cold-called may be abusive and rude if they resent the intrusion of an unwanted phone call. It is difficult for staff to deal with this all day and they need a supportive environment to help them cope.

The turnover of staff in call centres is often high, so the manager may spend a lot of time recruiting and training new staff. It is a challenging environment to work in and to manage. A good call centre, though, can be very successful. Income is often related to the number of sales or calls processed, so the manager of a successful centre can earn a lot.

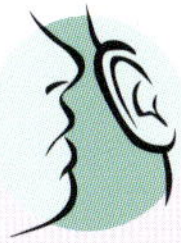

HANDY HINT

Some call centres are based abroad, so there may be the chance to work overseas. Some young people fund travel by working for a while in a call centre in India or elsewhere. This type of experience can help you gain a position in a call centre as a trainee manager. Most call centre managers begin as call centre workers and work their way up.

On Your Own

A career in retail doesn't always mean working for a large organisation. Some people work in small family shops, set up their own shop or run a market stall. The internet has provided a great opportunity for people to start their own retail businesses online, too.

ONLINE SELLER

It can be very expensive to set up a shop – but it costs very little to set up an online store. Many people who would love to have their own shop but can't raise the money or can't afford to give up their regular job set up online shops. There are many advantages: you don't have to work regular hours, you don't need to pay for premises and staff, and you can attract customers from around the world rather than rely on people who are physically nearby walking into your shop.

Many people who set up an online shop do so because they make their own products, or have a passion for a particular type of product. Their stock may be a minority interest with a market too spread out for a physical shop. Or they may run their online shop as a hobby or for extra income while studying or working at another job.

Small shopkeepers often rely on a combination of passing trade and online sales.

Kathryn – online shopkeeper

'I have an online shop selling antique French fabrics. I am passionate about old fabrics, and I dreamed for years of having a little shop to sell them, but I live in a remote area of Wales and I would have had to move – no one would find my shop here! Selling online is perfect for me. I have some regular customers in the USA and Canada, and I often sell to interior designers working on restoring old houses in France. I've sold quite a bit to people making films, too.

Searching for fabrics. The internet is a perfect vehicle for owners of small businesses.

'I buy my fabrics in France. I go over for a couple of weeks at a time and tour the antique fairs, flea markets, old junk shops and auctions. I collect vast quantities of fabric and bring it all back in my car. Some needs cleaning or restoring, and sometimes I have to unpick clothes or other items to reclaim the fabric. Then I photograph everything and write a description of it, including where it's from and its date. It's very different for customers buying fabric online as they can't feel it, so I have to provide as much other information as possible.

'My prices are lower online than they would be if I had to rent a shop and employ staff. The price has to cover postage, of course, but that works out less than the other overheads would have been.

'Of course, I don't meet customers like I would in a real shop. But I've made online friendships with some of my regular customers, and I've learnt what they like and are interested in. If I pick up something I know will be perfect for one of my customers, I email them immediately and offer it before I put it in the shop. That's not something you can do in a real shop, and the customers really appreciate it. It's very rewarding – I'm working with a product I love and dealing with like-minded people who share my passion for it. I wouldn't change it for the world.'

MARKET STALL HOLDER

Several people who went on to build great business or retail empires started life as 'barrow boys' selling things from a market stall. Traditional market stalls sell anything from fruit and vegetables to craft items and cheap household goods. Some people choose to run a market stall because they make or grow their own products and want to sell them; others are excited by the challenge of buying goods cheaply and selling them quickly to make a profit. Running a market stall is hard physical work. You may need to move your stock to and from the stall every day, and you will have to open and close the stall, perhaps even building it and taking it apart each day. If your stall is outside, you will need stamina and good health as you will be working in all weathers.

Market stall holders have more freedom than shop employees but they need to be fit, as they are outdoors in all weathers.

WHAT TO SELL?

If you want a market stall to sell something you grow or make yourself, you will need to make sure you have enough stock. You probably won't open your stall every day, as you will spend a lot of time collecting stock. But if you buy your stock – whether from farmers or wholesalers – you may be on the stall every day. Some products are seasonal and you might need different suppliers to provide slightly different products over the year. If you have a clothes stall, for instance, you might sell jumpers and coats in winter but shorts and swimwear in summer.

TO RUN A MARKET STALL, YOU WILL NEED

- ***confidence***
- ***an outgoing personality***
- ***good health and physical fitness***

BLUFF AND BLUSTER

The traditional image of a market stallholder is of a loud, brash person who shouts to passersby, trying to get them to stop and look at the products. Most market stallholders are not like this any more, but they still need confidence and an outgoing personality.

You will need good interpersonal skills to work on a market stall as you will be dealing with members of the public every day. You will also be working alongside other stall holders and dealing with your suppliers. You will need the confidence to haggle, too – many people expect to negotiate prices with a market stallholder. You will need to negotiate prices with your suppliers.

An Italian fruit stall holder: market stall work is often carried out by families and continued from one generation to the next.

HANDY HINT

You will need to do some careful research and calculations to set your prices so that you still make a profit but manage to attract enough customers. There might be some trial and error involved. If you sell all your stock very easily, you might be able to charge more; if sales are slow, you will do better to drop your prices and sell more.

TO RUN YOUR OWN SHOP, YOU WILL NEED

- *to be versatile – there are lots of different tasks to cover*
- *to be physically fit, as you will need to lift and move stock*
- *knowledge of the shop's stock and customer requirements*

INDEPENDENT SHOPKEEPER

You may choose to set up your own shop if you create a product or have a particular passion for some kind of product – or because you love the idea of having a shop. Running a shop is hard work, involving long hours. It can be high risk, as independent shops have to compete with big traders with a large workforce and more finance. When you start out, you will have to carry out all the tasks yourself, including organisation, finance, administration, buying, marketing and promotion as well as stocking the shop and selling to customers.

RESEARCH

Researching products, competitors, suppliers and prices before you start is vital. You will also need to work out where to set up your shop. Will it depend on passing trade, or will people be prepared to go out of their way to find it? How will you promote it, letting people know it exists?

FINANCE

Setting up a shop is expensive. You may have savings or be able to borrow from your family, but many entrepreneurs take out a business loan from a bank. To do this, you will need to put together a business plan and work out the costings – how much it will cost to rent premises, employ staff, buy stock, pay bills, and support yourself while your business gets going. Your research into products and suppliers and the viability of your business will feed into your business plan.

Independent shopkeeping is a risky business, but it can result in big financial rewards.

Getting to know your customers well is one of the most rewarding aspects of retail work.

WORKING ALONE

To work for yourself you need to be motivated, to be able to manage your time, and be willing to turn your hand to any task. It can be very stressful as well as very exciting. Anyone working on their own needs to deal with their own accounts, including completing tax returns. You will need to keep all the receipts and other documents that you will need. You might want an accountant to help you with your accounts.

IS RETAIL RIGHT FOR YOU?

Retail is an exciting and lively sector of the economy. If you want to work in a vibrant environment, having contact with lots of people and dealing with a product range you love, retail can be very rewarding. There are so many roles available in retail that there is something to suit almost everyone. As with any career choice, it is important to research the area you are interested in thoroughly so that you make an informed decision that will set you on the path to a happy and successful working life.

HANDY HINT

Working in a small independent shop can give you a great introduction to all the tasks involved before you set up your own business. You may gain experience of buying, visual merchandising, promotion, stock control, customer service, finance, and other aspects of working in retail.

Further Information

BOOKS

Careers in Retail (Wetfeet Insider Guides), Wetfeet, 2008

Columbo, George W. **Start your Retail Career (Pocket Guides on Careers)**, Entrepreneur Press, 2008

O'Malley, Stephanie **Start your Retail Career**, Entrepreneur Press, 2009

Retail (Ferguson's Careers in Focus), Ferguson Publishing, 2007

Stinson, Paul **Top Careers in Two Years: Retail, Marketing, and Sales**, Facts On File Inc., 2008

WEBSITES

www.acareerinretail.co.uk
A Career in Retail website with over 50 articles and case studies.

www.allretailjobs.com
A retail job board listing thousands of job opportunities.

www.bls.gov
The US Bureau of Labour Statistics site with information about job openings.

www.graduatetoretail.org
Information on graduate careers in retail.

www.inretail.co.uk/pages/content.asp
A recruitment website for the retail industry.

www.nrf.com
The website of the National Retail Federation.

www.retailcareers.co.uk/pages/content.asp
UK website listing career opportunities in retail.

www.retailmoves.com
Retail moves careers website.

www.skillsmartretail.com
Skillsmart Retail website, with information about retail skills development.

Glossary

auctioneer a person who announces the lots and controls the bidding at an auction (a public sale of property or goods)

barcode a code made up of numbers and lines that can be read by a till at a checkout; it registers the price of goods and helps to record the amount of stock left in the store

bric-a-brac a variety of small objects, usually furniture and other collectable items, sold on the basis that they are unusual or decorative

CIMA Chartered Institute of Management Accountants

co-operative an organisation owned and run by its workers for their joint benefit

deteriorate become gradually worse in quality

footfall the number of people passing through a shop at any one time

haulage transportation of goods for commercial purposes

human resources also known as 'personnel', this refers to the department of a company or organisation responsible for hiring and training staff

humidity dampness, or the measure of the amount of moisture in the air

interior design a profession that involves planning the decoration and furnishings inside a house or shop

logistics planning and organising the movement of goods from one place to another

merchandising goods sold in a shop, or the promotion of goods to be sold

payroll a list of people employed by a company, with details of how much each person is paid

perishable food that is likely to rot quickly

psychology the scientific study of the human mind and the way in which it works

retail chain a group of shops owned by the same company

rota a list of names giving the order in which employees take their turn to carry out certain tasks

statistical describes the use of statistics – data obtained from the study of a large amount of numerical information

stock the supply of goods available for sale in a store

warehouse a large building where goods are stored and from where they are transported to shops for sale, or mailed direct to the customer, in the case of internet shopping

warranty a written guarantee, given to a person when he or she buys a product, promising to replace or repair it if necessary within a limited period of time

Index

Numbers in **bold** refer to illustrations.